The Twelve Days of Christmas

Illustrated by Violeta Dabija

On the first day of Christmas, my true love sent to me,

a partridge in a pear tree.

On the second day of Christmas,
my true love sent to me,

two turtle doves

and a partridge
in a pear tree.

On the third day of Christmas,
my true love sent to me,

three French hens,

two turtle doves
and a partridge in a pear tree.

On the fourth day of Christmas,
my true love sent to me,

four calling birds,

three French hens,
two turtle doves
and a partridge in a pear tree.

On the fifth day of Christmas,
my true love sent to me,

five gold rings,

four calling birds,
three French hens,
two turtle doves
and a partridge in a pear tree.

On the sixth day of Christmas,
my true love sent to me,

six geese a-laying,

five gold rings,
four calling birds,
three French hens,
two turtle doves
and a partridge in a pear tree.

On the seventh day of Christmas,
my true love sent to me,

seven swans a-swimming,

six geese a-laying,
five gold rings,
four calling birds,
three French hens,
two turtle doves
and a partridge in a pear tree.

On the eighth day of Christmas, my true love sent to me,

eight maids a-milking,

seven swans a-swimming, six geese a-laying, five gold rings,
four calling birds, three French hens, two turtle doves
and a partridge in a pear tree.

On the ninth day of Christmas,
my true love sent to me,

nine ladies dancing,

eight maids a-milking,
seven swans a-swimming,
six geese a-laying,
five gold rings,
four calling birds,
three French hens,
two turtle doves
and a partridge in a pear tree.

On the tenth day of Christmas, my true love sent to me,
ten lords a-leaping,

nine ladies dancing, eight maids a-milking,
seven swans a-swimming, six geese a-laying,
five gold rings, four calling birds, three French hens,
two turtle doves and a partridge in a pear tree.

On the eleventh day of Christmas,
my true love sent to me,

eleven pipers piping,

ten lords a-leaping,
nine ladies dancing,
eight maids a-milking,
seven swans a-swimming,
six geese a-laying,
five gold rings,
four calling birds,
three French hens,
two turtle doves
and a partridge in a pear tree.

On the twelfth day of Christmas, my true love sent to me,

twelve drummers drumming,

eleven pipers piping,
ten lords a-leaping,
nine ladies dancing,
eight maids a-milking,
seven swans a-swimming,
six geese a-laying,
five gold rings,
four calling birds,
three French hens,
two turtle doves
and a partridge in a pear tree.

Designed by Caroline Spatz
Edited by Lesley Sims

This edition first published in 2015 by Usborne Publishing Ltd., Usborne House, 83-85 Saffron Hill, London EC1N 8RT, England.
www.usborne.com Copyright © 2015, 2012 Usborne Publishing Ltd.